Carving Wooden Critters

by

Diane (Ernst) Harto

Fox Chapel
PUBLISHING

ISBN 978-1-56523-771-1

To learn more about the other great books from Fox Chapel Publishing,
or to find a retailer near you, call toll-free 800-457-9112, or visit us at
www.FoxChapelPublishing.com.

We are always looking for talented authors. To submit an idea, please send a brief inquiry to
acquisitions@foxchapelpublishing.com.

Printed in the USA

Table of Contents

Foreword

The patterns and instructions in this book are for use by carvers of all levels of skill.

When I carve, I use a Foredom® flexible shaft power tool from start to finish, so my comments and suggestions will be referring to this method of carving. Of course, these ideas may be applied to any method of carving you choose.

The wood I prefer is Basswood. Its clean, white color and lack of grain make it ideal, in my opinion, for this type of work. I also like the way it takes wood burning.

Most of the carvings shown in this book are finished with wood burning. I don't usually do anything else to the piece because this is the way I like my carvings to look. However, I would encourage you to experiment with paints and other types of finishes to see what you like best.

When I set out to draw a pattern, one of my goals is not to attain photographic realism, but to bring out the charm and character of the subject. I want my carvings to grab the eye and create the urge to touch. I believe that 90 percent of the character is found (or lost) in a carving's facial expression. On one occasion at a carving show, a gentleman picked up one of my bears to get a better look. "When you look at his face, you get a surprise," he said. Then he bought it!

As you start to carve, the most important goal you should have is to please yourself! With that in mind, let's see how you do.

Techniques and Tools

1 Mark a blank with pencil to show where and how to start shaping.

2 Mark these guidelines on the back of the blank as well.

3 Use a large cone-shape burr to shape the bunny. Be sure to turn and work all sides of the bunny.

4 Reapply the pencil marks for the eyes, nose and mouth as you carve. You'll find that placement of the facial features is easier this way.

5 When your carving looks like this, changet o a smaller,t aperedb urr. Use a sphericalb urrt o hollowt he ears.

6

A back view of the roughly shaped bunny.

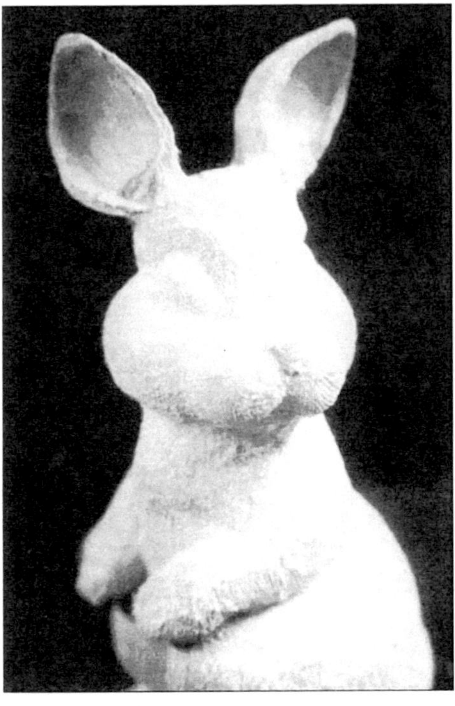

7 With the tapered burr, cut in the outline of your bunny's eyes, nose, mouth and limbs. Don't be afraid to cut fairly deep.

8 Still using the small burr, round off the edges of your outlines.

9

Now begin sanding. Use a sanding drum with 220 grit paper. Carefully sand away all burr marks. In places where your drum doesn't fit, use a skinny mandrel with 220 grit. Pencil the details in again.

10 Using a tear-shape diamond cutter, cut in outlines for eyes, nose, mouth and limbs as you did before. This time, show a separation between the eyeballs and eyelids. Using the same cutter, refine these details carefully. Keep checking for balance in the eyes.

11 Change to a needle-shaped diamond cutter. Use this cutter to sharpen eyelids and nostrils, and to indicate toes. Use a cylinder-shaped diamond cutter to texture the tail. Hold the cutter at an angle so only the edge touches. Clean up the "fuzz" with sandpaper.

12 Time to do the final sanding. Start with the mandrel to remove any remaining tool marks, then switch to hand-held 220 grit paper. S nding takes time! Continue to sand until the wood is smooth all over. The better you sand, the better your burning will come out later.

13 Pencili n the fur pattern. Pay attention to the direction in which the fur lies; it follows the curves of the body. A dog or a cat is a goode xample . Mark dark and light areas, as well as direction.

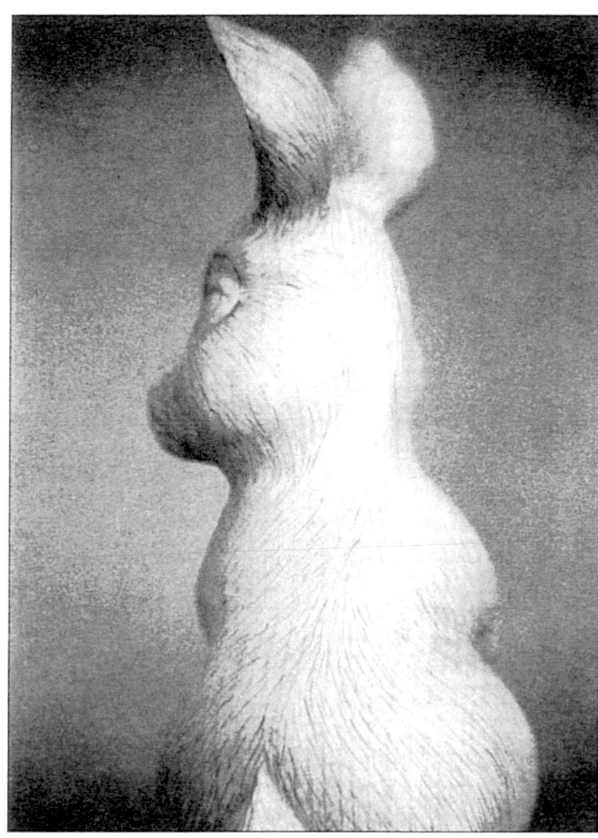

14 This view of the bunny shows the fur pattern on the bunny's back.

15 Start burning the nose and eyes by laying the burner point flat on the surface of the wood. Slide it carefully over the wood, creating a shiny, leathery feeling. Keep the tool moving to avoid flat marks. Start burning on the fur at the nose using short straight strokes. As you work toward areas where the fur is longer, use longer, curved strokes. Leave the light areas for later.

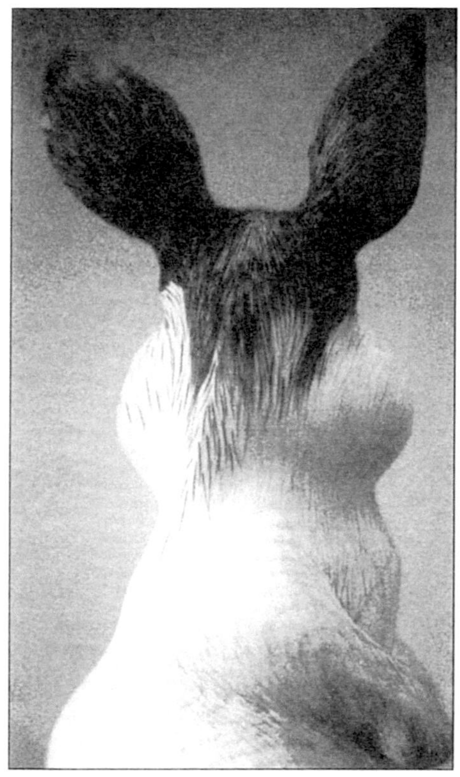

16 The burn marks on the back of the bunny's head will look like this.

17 Continue on this way following your guidelines until the dark fur areas are filled in.

18 Turn down the setting on your burner and, with a very light touch, fill in the light areas. To burn the tail, use a low setting and the same techniques you used in Step 15. Nice job!

Finishing Tips

PANDA

To give the panda its fur texture, I start with a cylinder-shaped diamond cutter and go over the entire animal, following my penciled guidelines. I clean up the "fuzz" with creased sandpaper or an old tooth brush. Then I wood burn the black areas with the wood burner set fairly high. The white areas will be more of a vanilla-white color, but I prefer this look to a painted one.

HARP SEAL

When I do carvings of sea creatures, I like to use butternut wood because of its beautiful grain. For the best results, I take special care to sand the surfaces very smooth, removing *all* tool marks. I use high gloss tung oil to finish this type of carving. It is best applied with a soft cloth. I use a small brush for harder to reach spots. After each coat of oil dries, I rub it down with very fine steel wool before applying the next coat. I'm usually satisfied with the shine after the fourth coat. I DO NOT steel wool after the last coat of tung oil.

PUPPIES

The puppies can be finished any number of ways. The ones pictured in this book were painted with acrylics. Wonderful effects can also be achieved through the use of stains. To create spotted puppies, use a dark stain for the spots and finish the piece with tung oil. A good stain will allow the wood's grain to show through.

ORNAMENTS

When carving these ornaments you can make them as plain or elaborate as you choose. They can be finished with stain or paints. To make a painted "flat," just cut out the shape from 1/4" or 1/8" wide wood, then sand and paint. Finish with varathane. For a more "crafted look," use 1" wide wood and carve "in the round," as you would a large carving. I then paint carefully and rub with steel wool for an aged effect. The rocking horse shown in this book was carved in the round with two separate rockers, painted with bright acrylic colors, and finished with varathane.

Tools

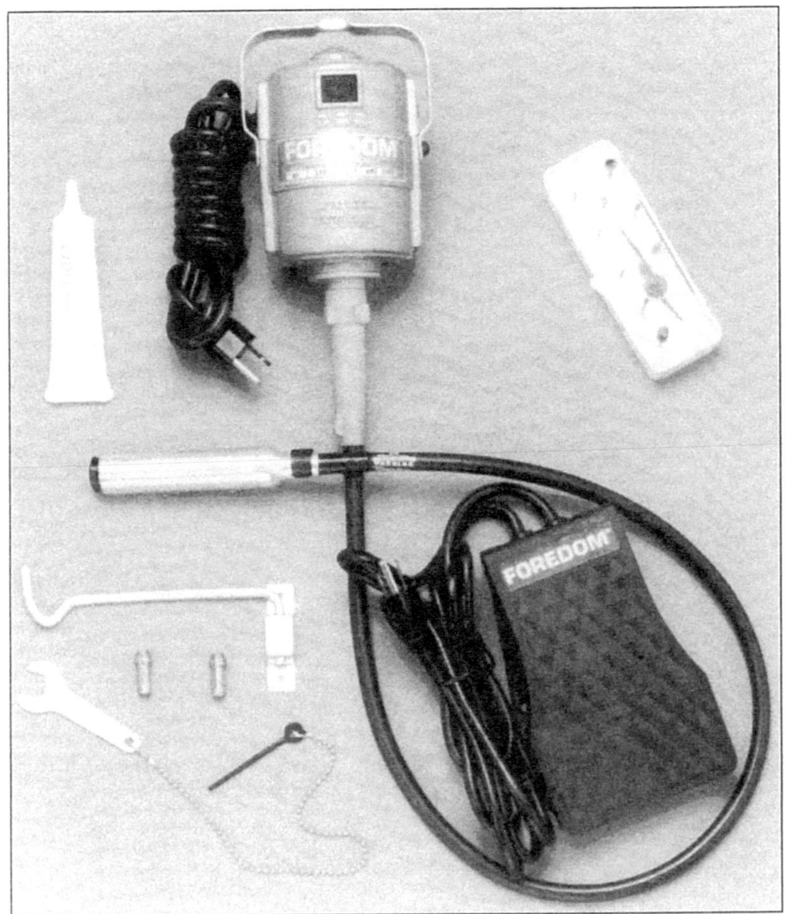

The Foredom Model 5240 Reversible is a popular flexibe shaft machine for power carvers.

A selection of popular burrs and tips for the power carver.
Back Row: Tear-shaped, carving twist drill, cone-shaped, ruby spherical burr, vanadium steel cutter.
Front Row: Three aluminum oxide points used for fine detailing, two red oxide points.

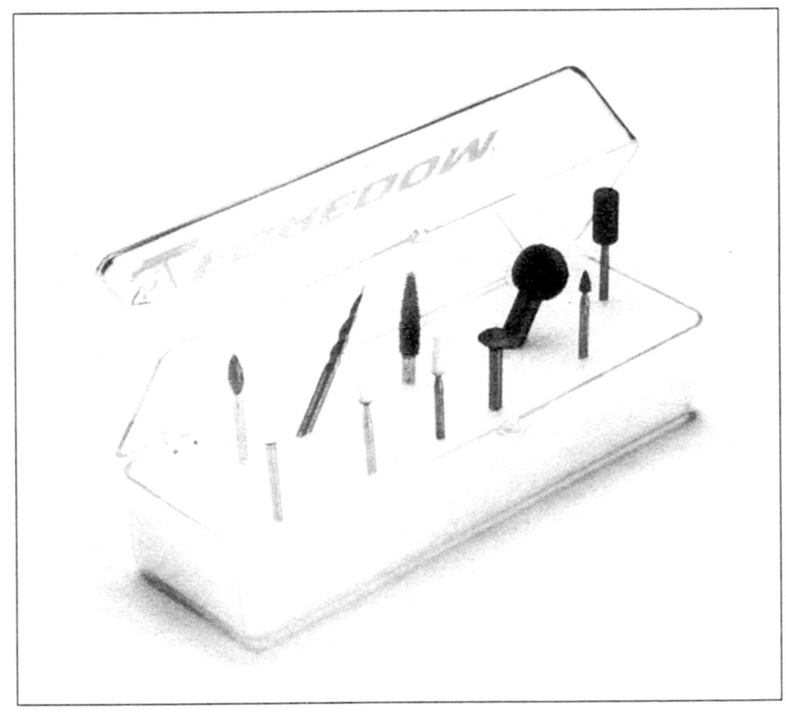

Patterns

Bunny Pattern

Taking a Break

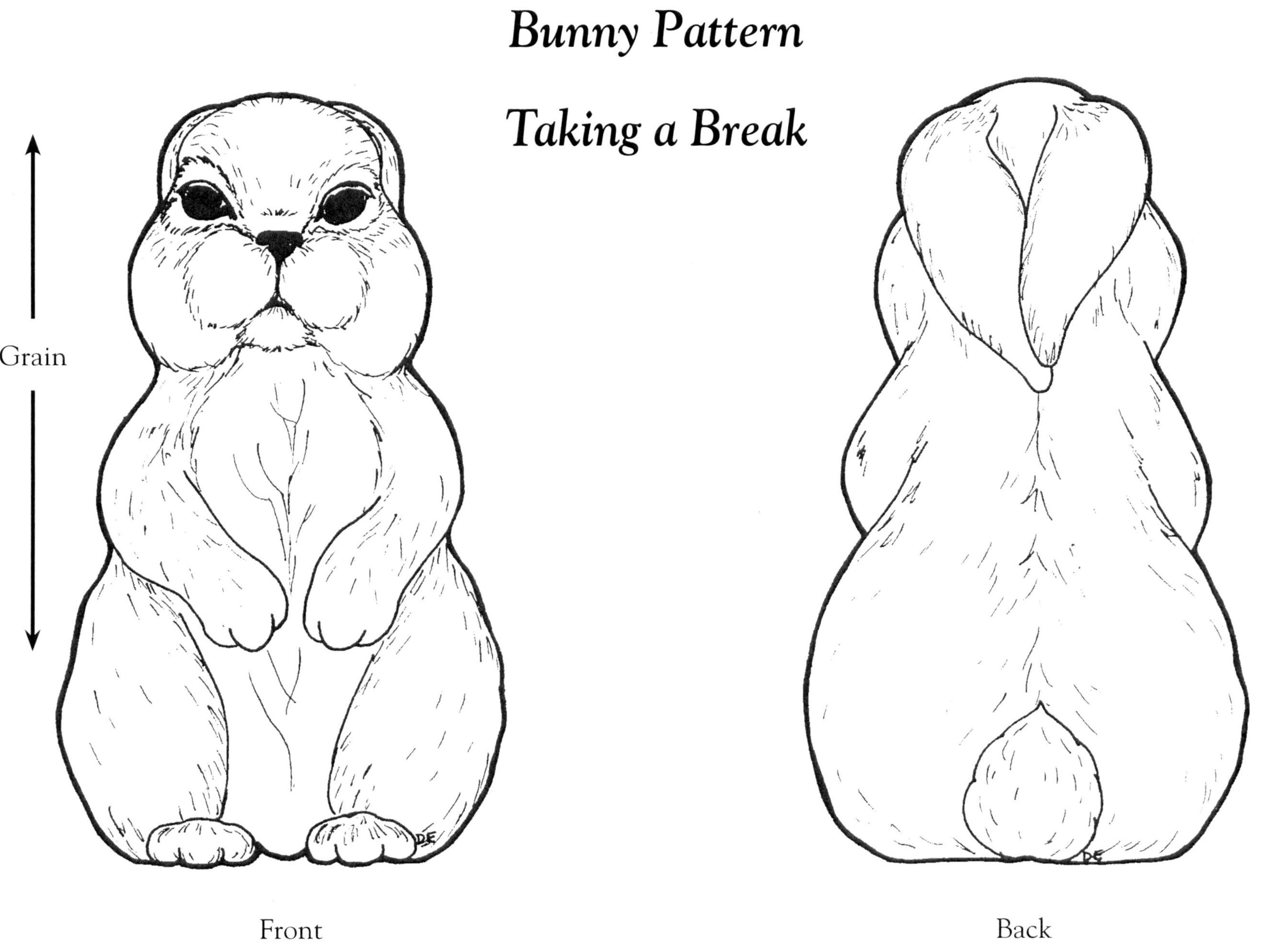

Carving Wooden Critters

Bunny Pattern

Taking a Break

Bunny Pattern

Napping Bunny

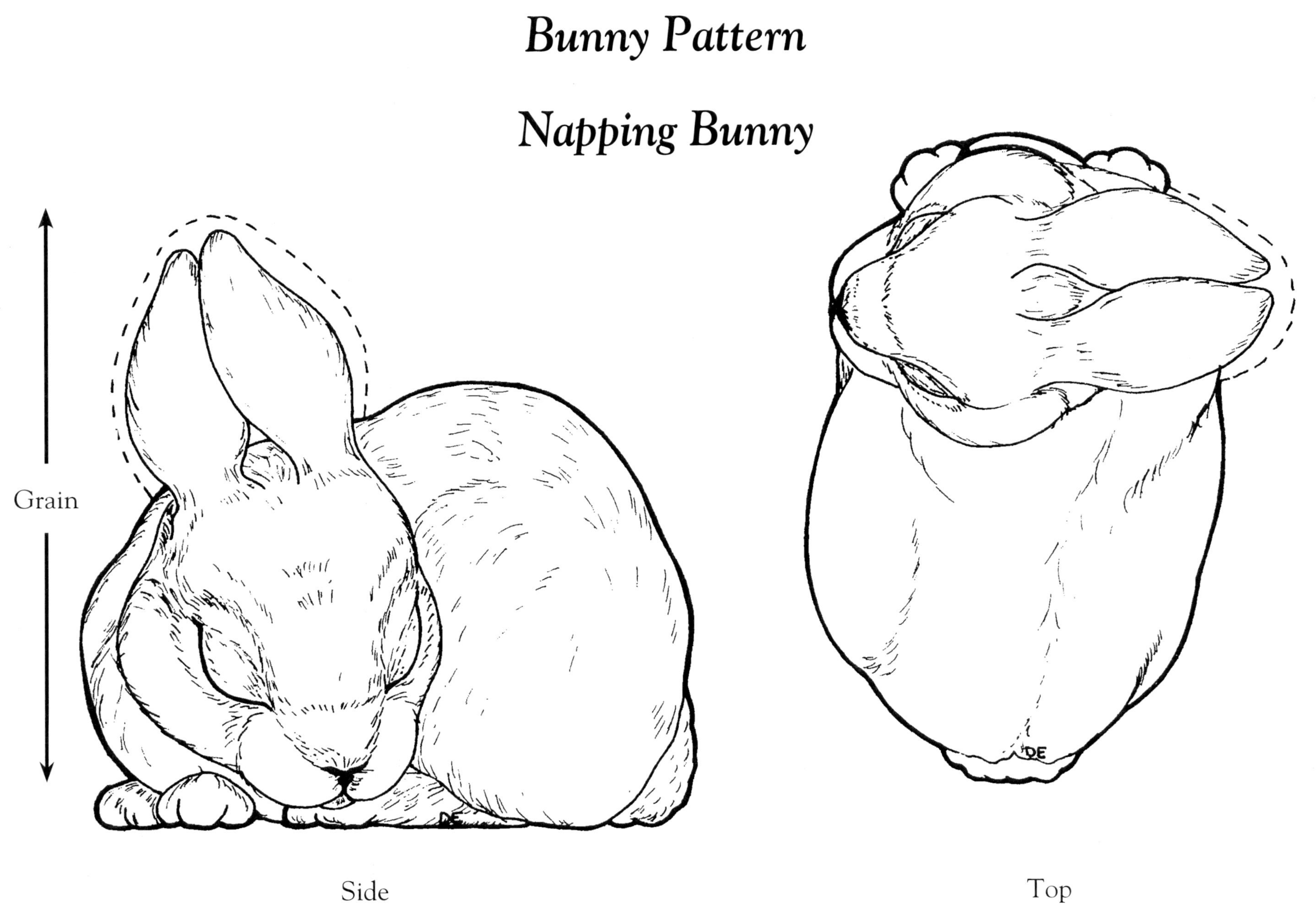

Bunny Pattern

Napping Bunny

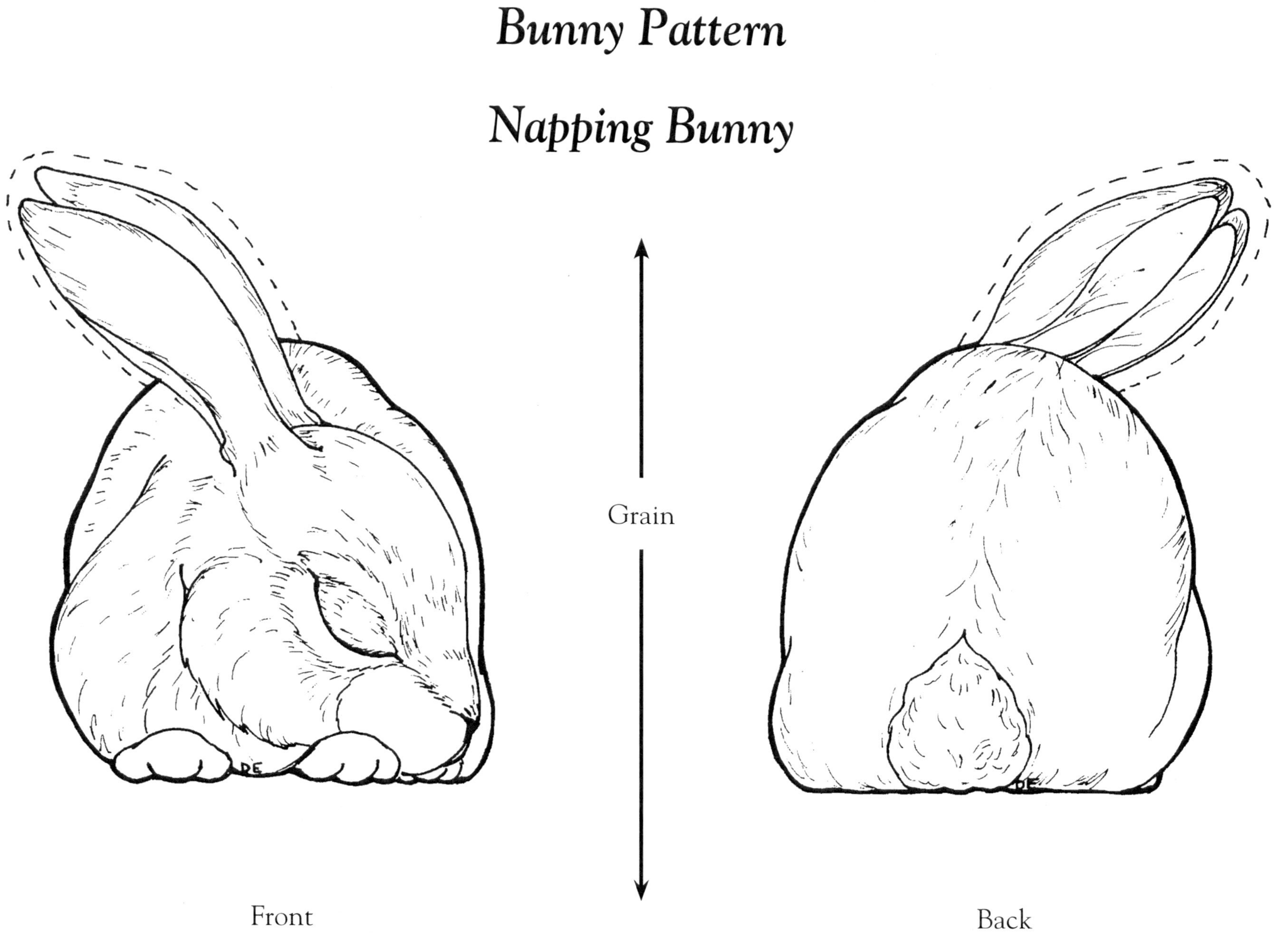

Bunny Pattern

Morning Bath

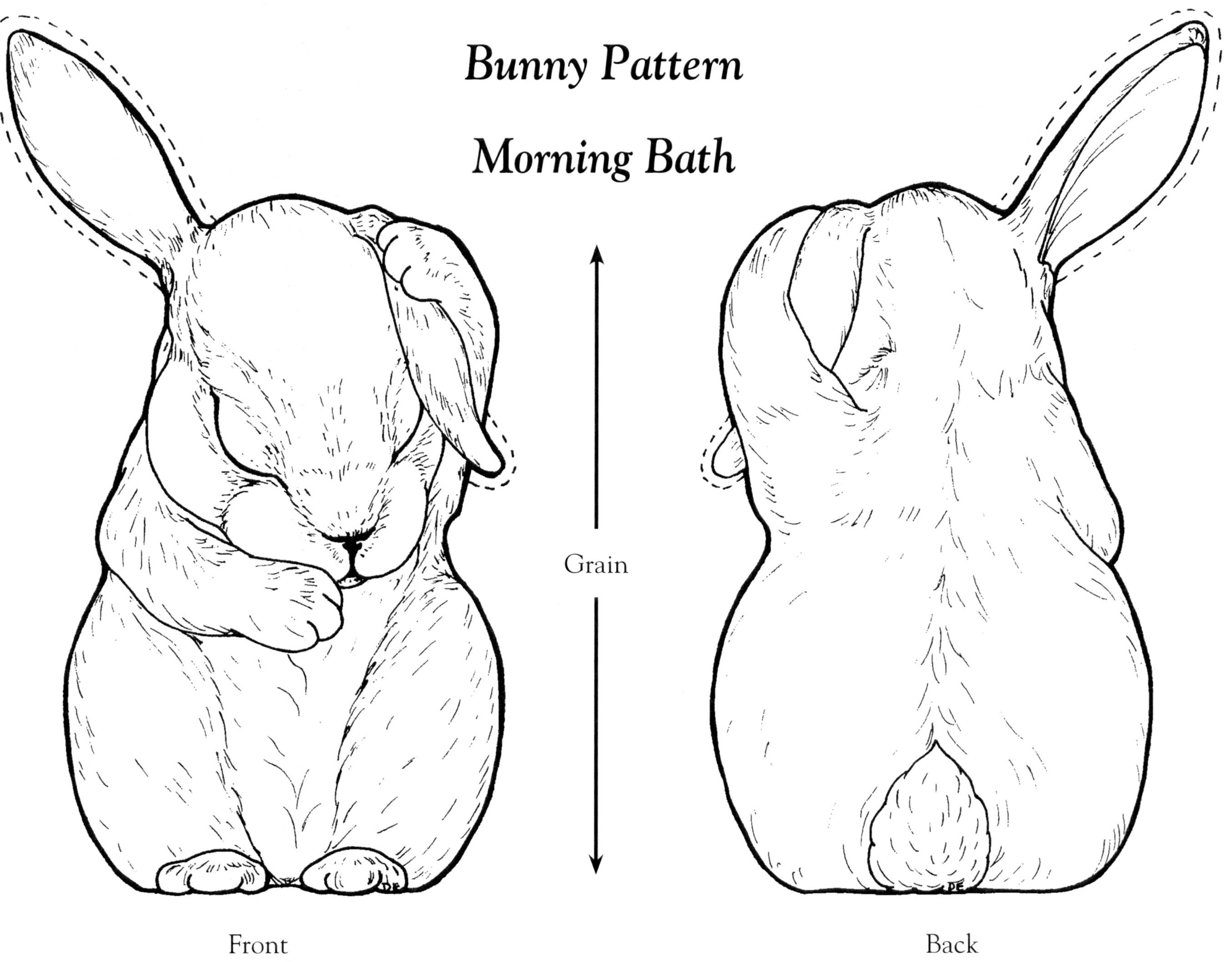

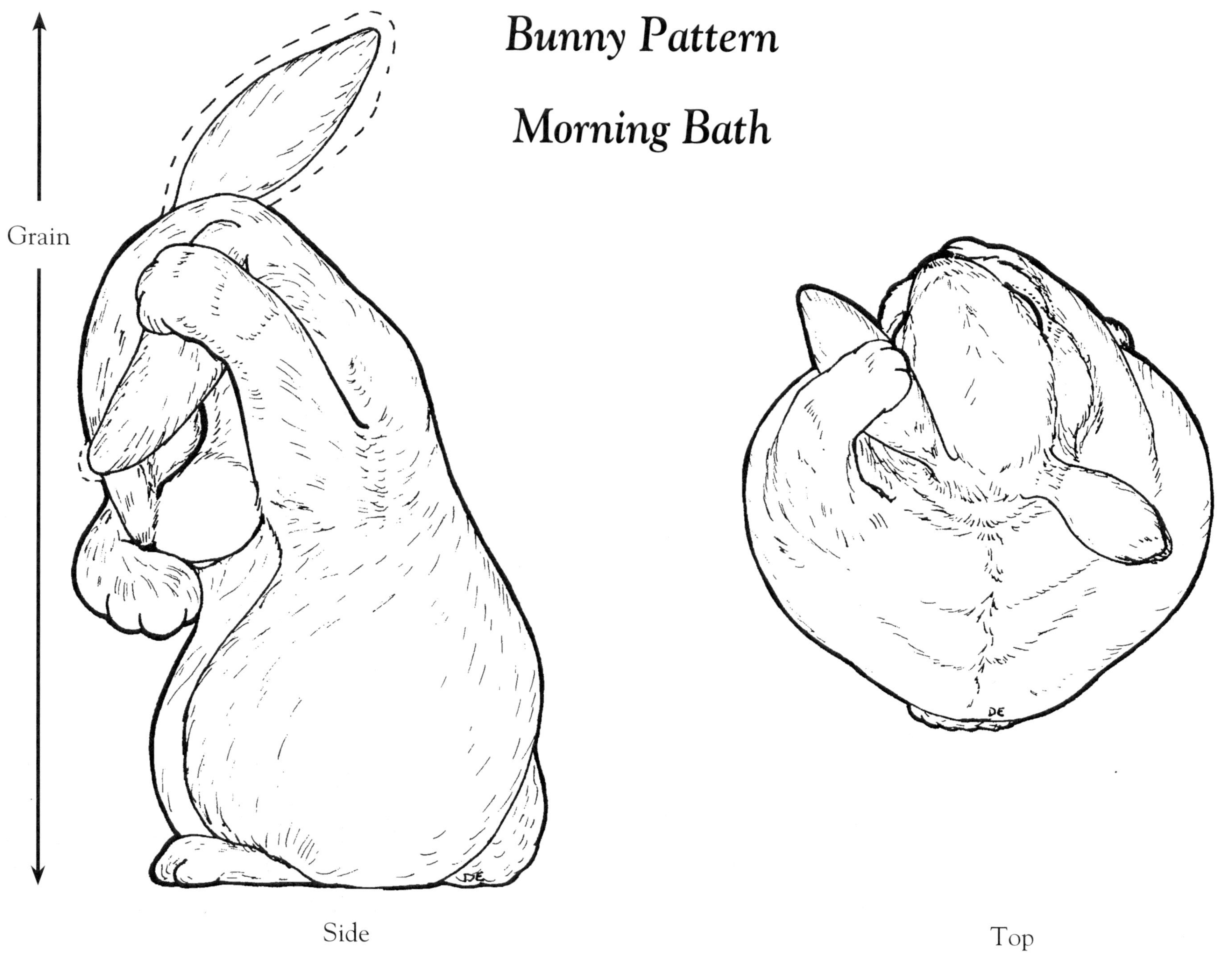

Bunny Pattern
Morning Bath
Grain
Side
Top

Bunny Pattern
Ready to Run
Leave extra wook around the ears.
Grain
Front
Back

Bunny Pattern

Ready to Run

Bunny Pattern
Freeze!

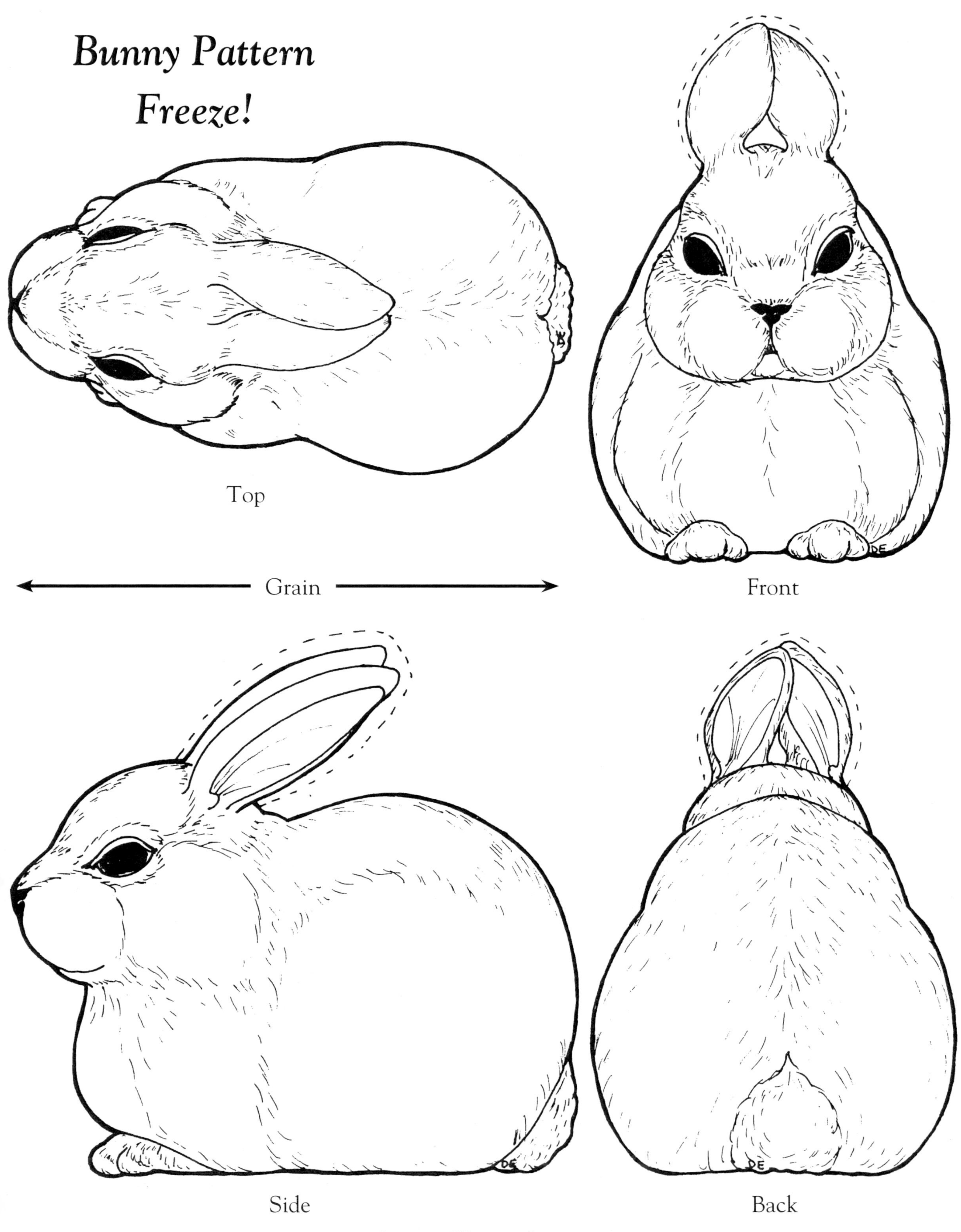

   Carving Wooden Critters

Puppy Pattern   Sloppy Kisser

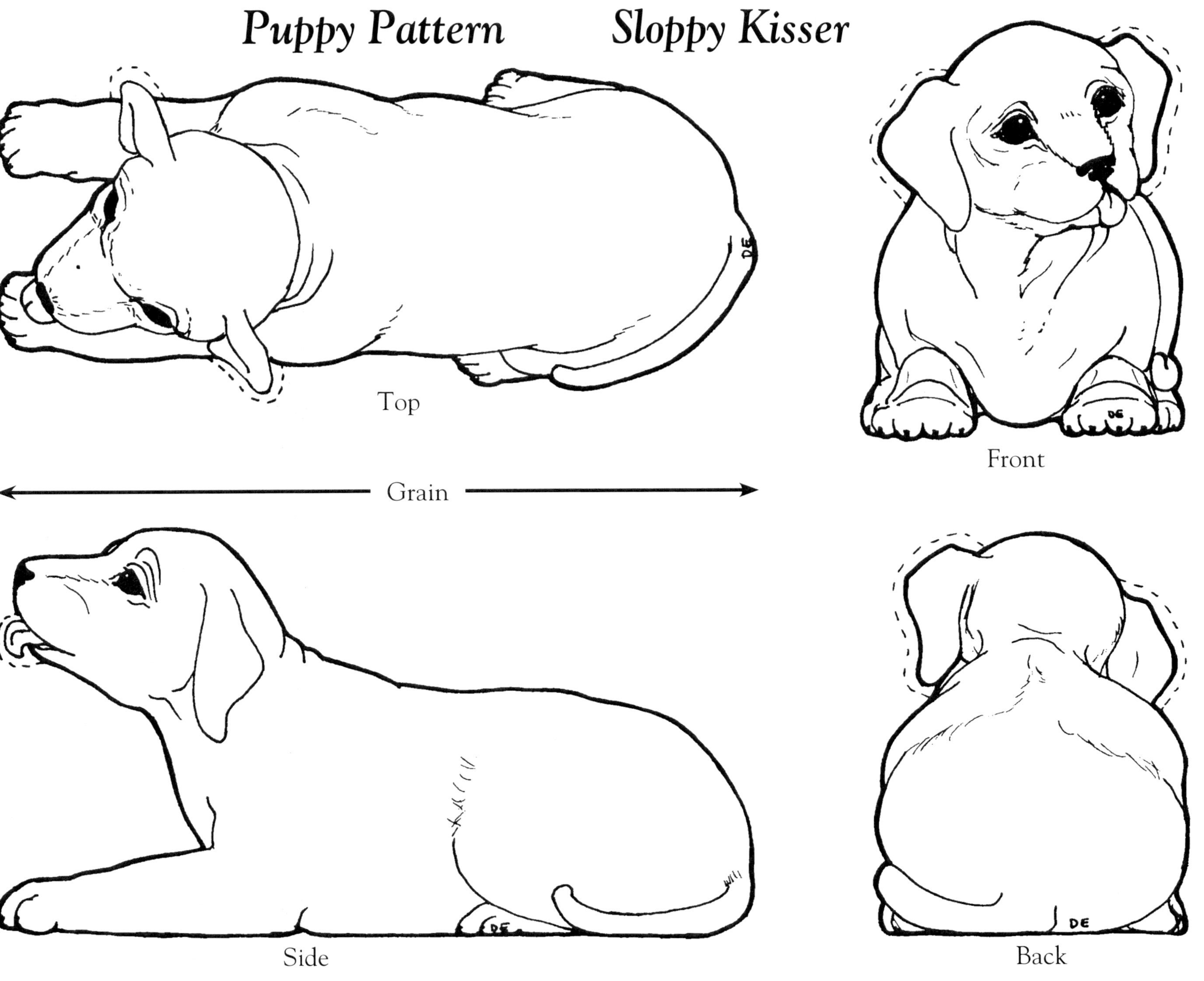

Puppy Pattern

Jr. Watch Dog

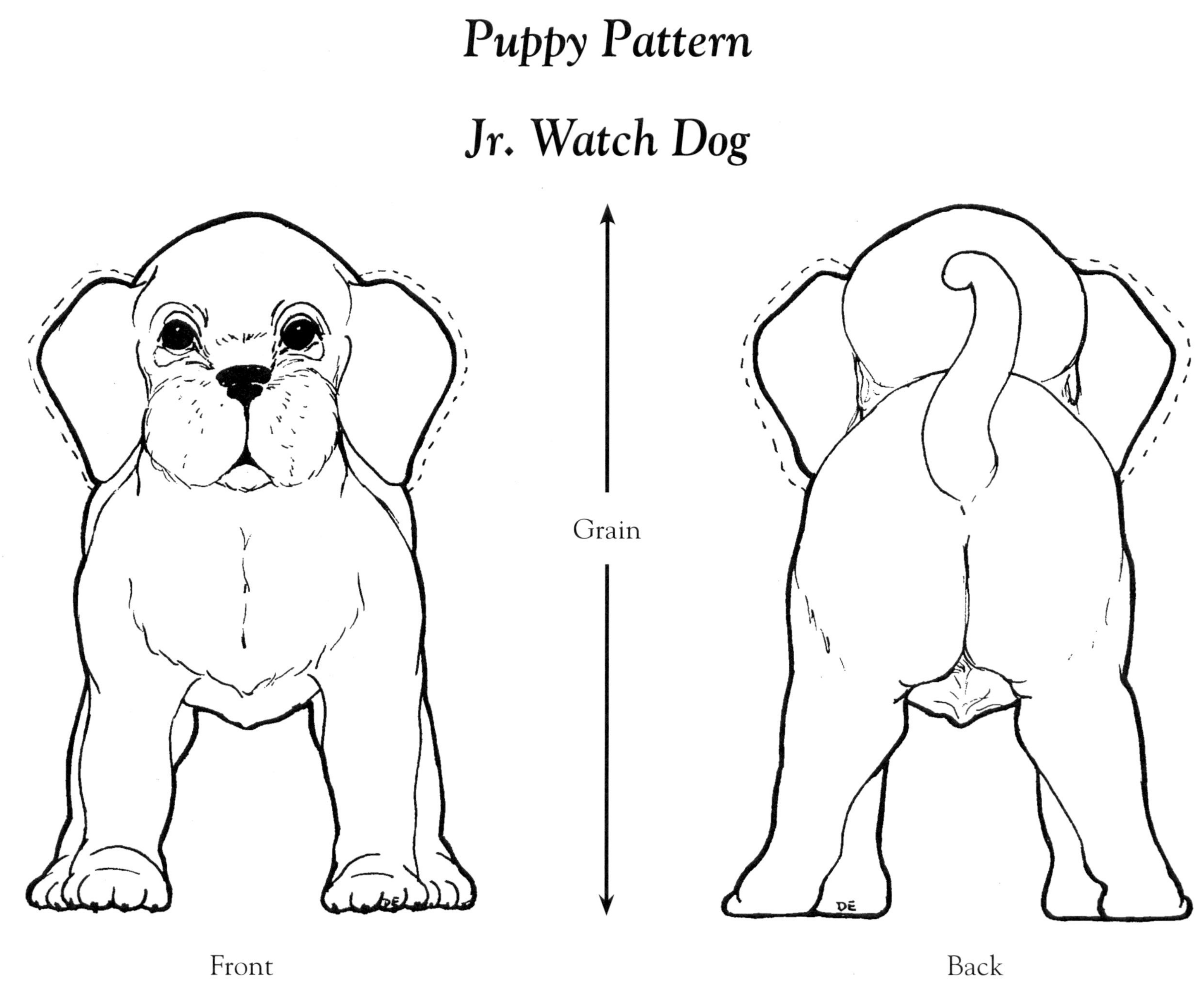

Puppy Pattern

Jr. Watch Dog

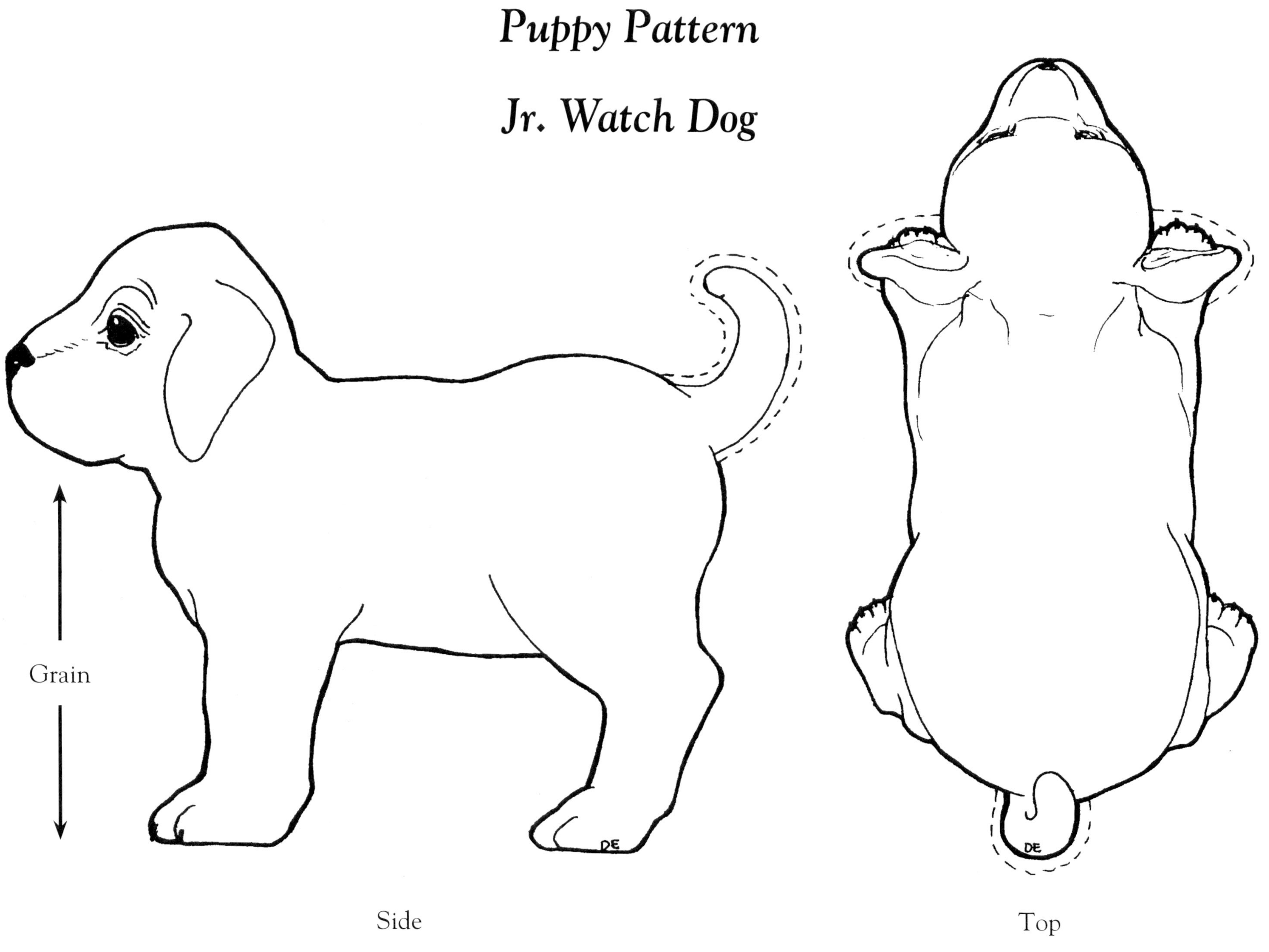

Puppy Pattern

Playful Pup

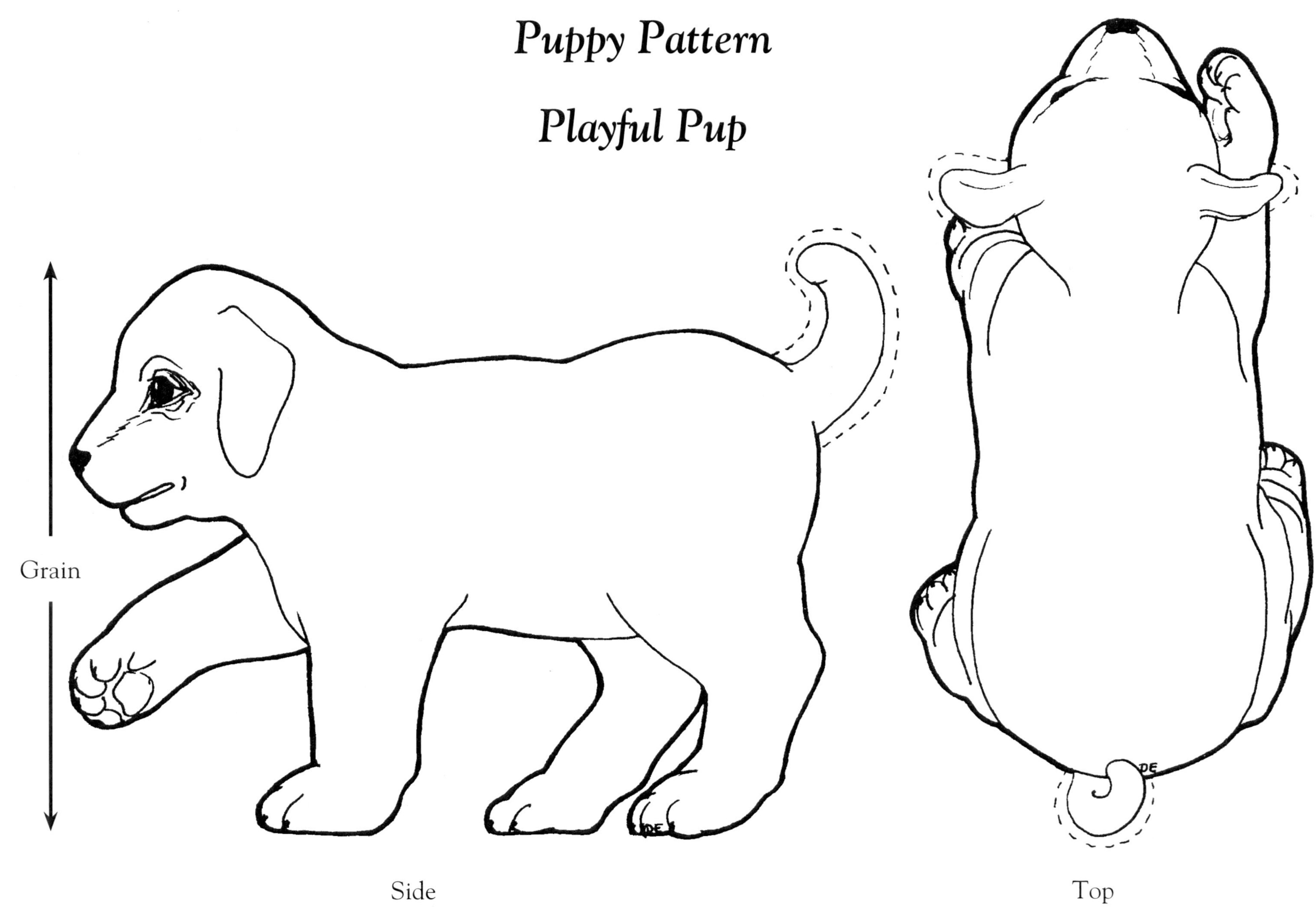

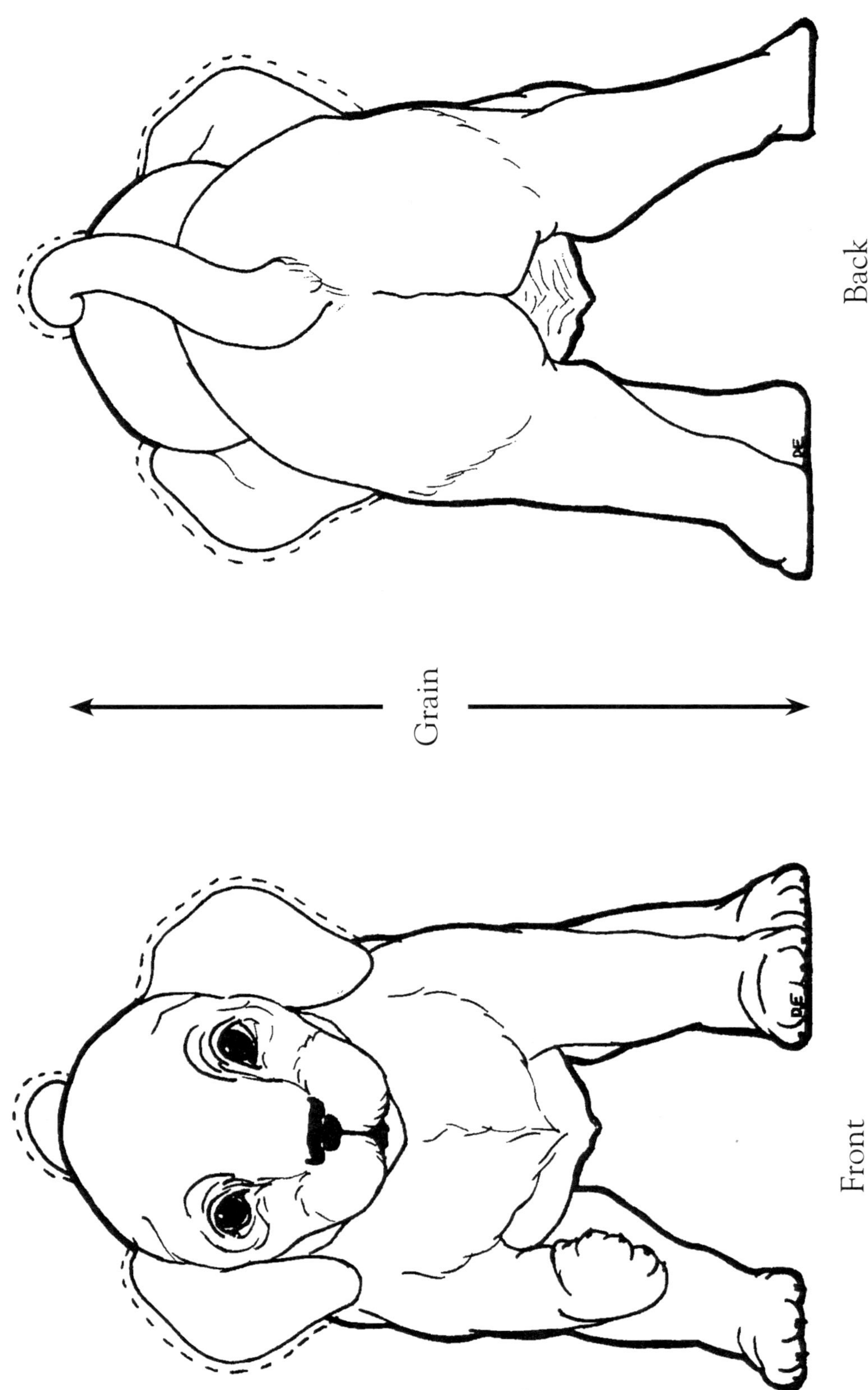

Puppy Pattern
Playful Pup
Back
Grain
Front

Puppy Pattern

Rainy Day Puppy

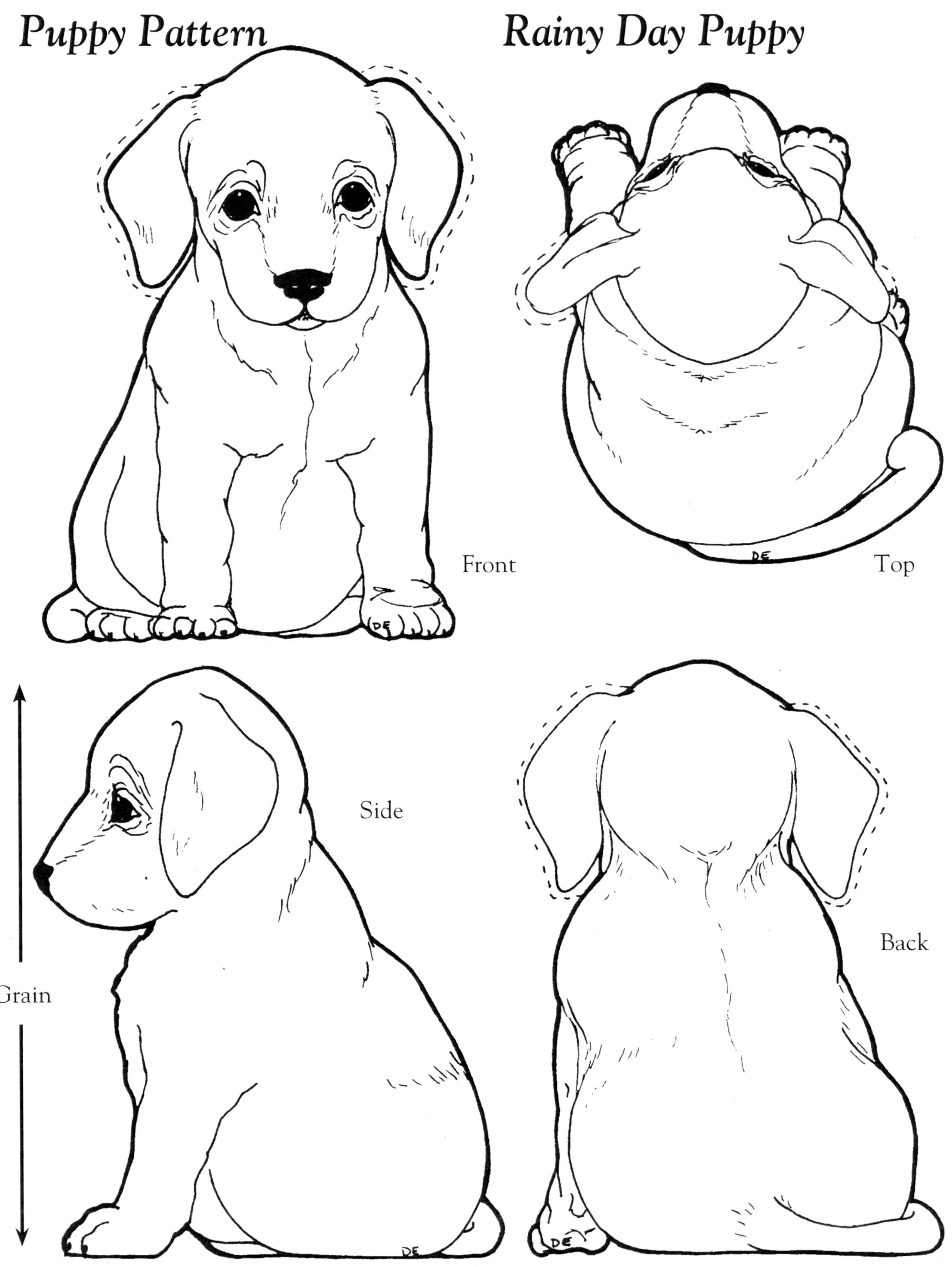

Carving Wooden Critters

Howler

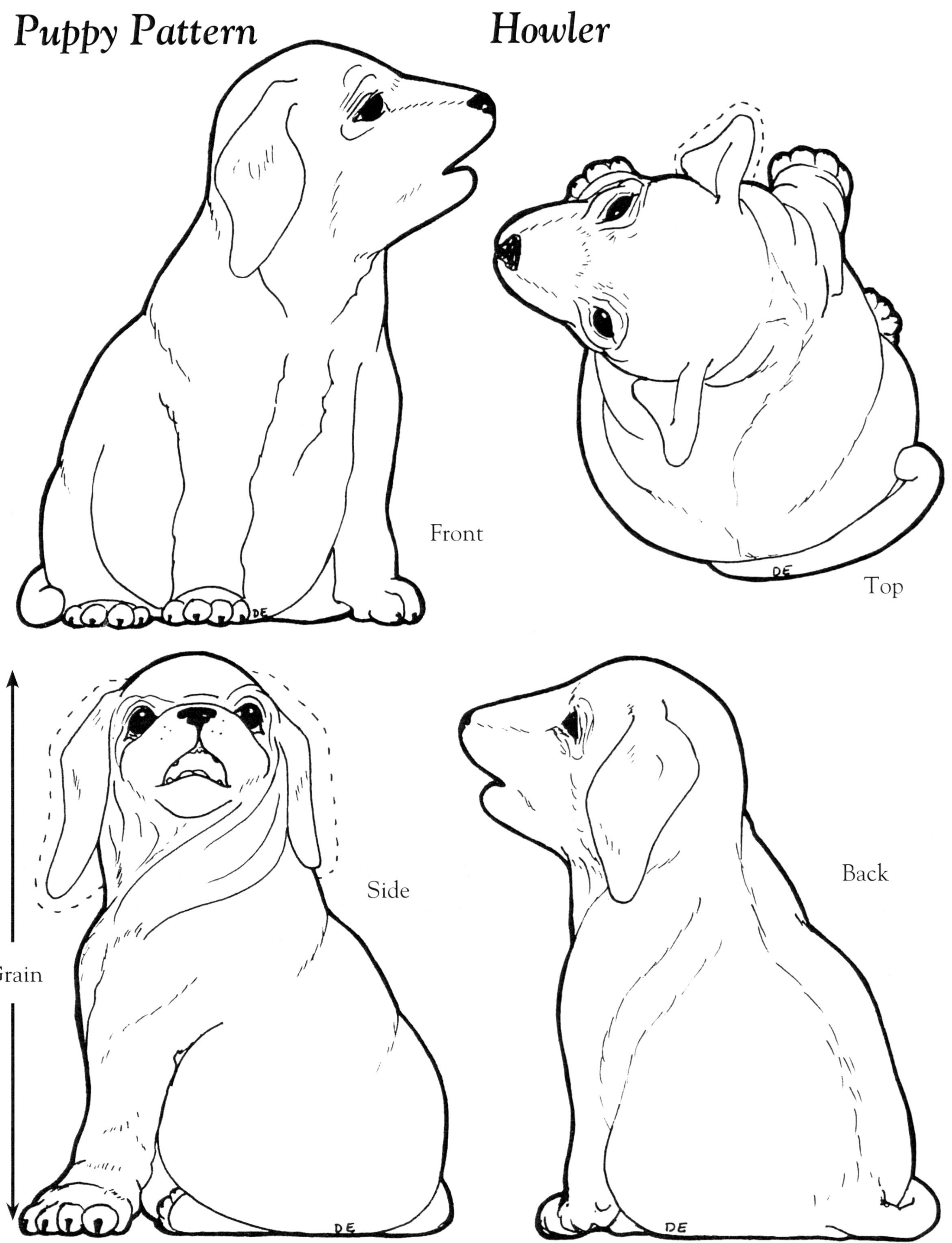

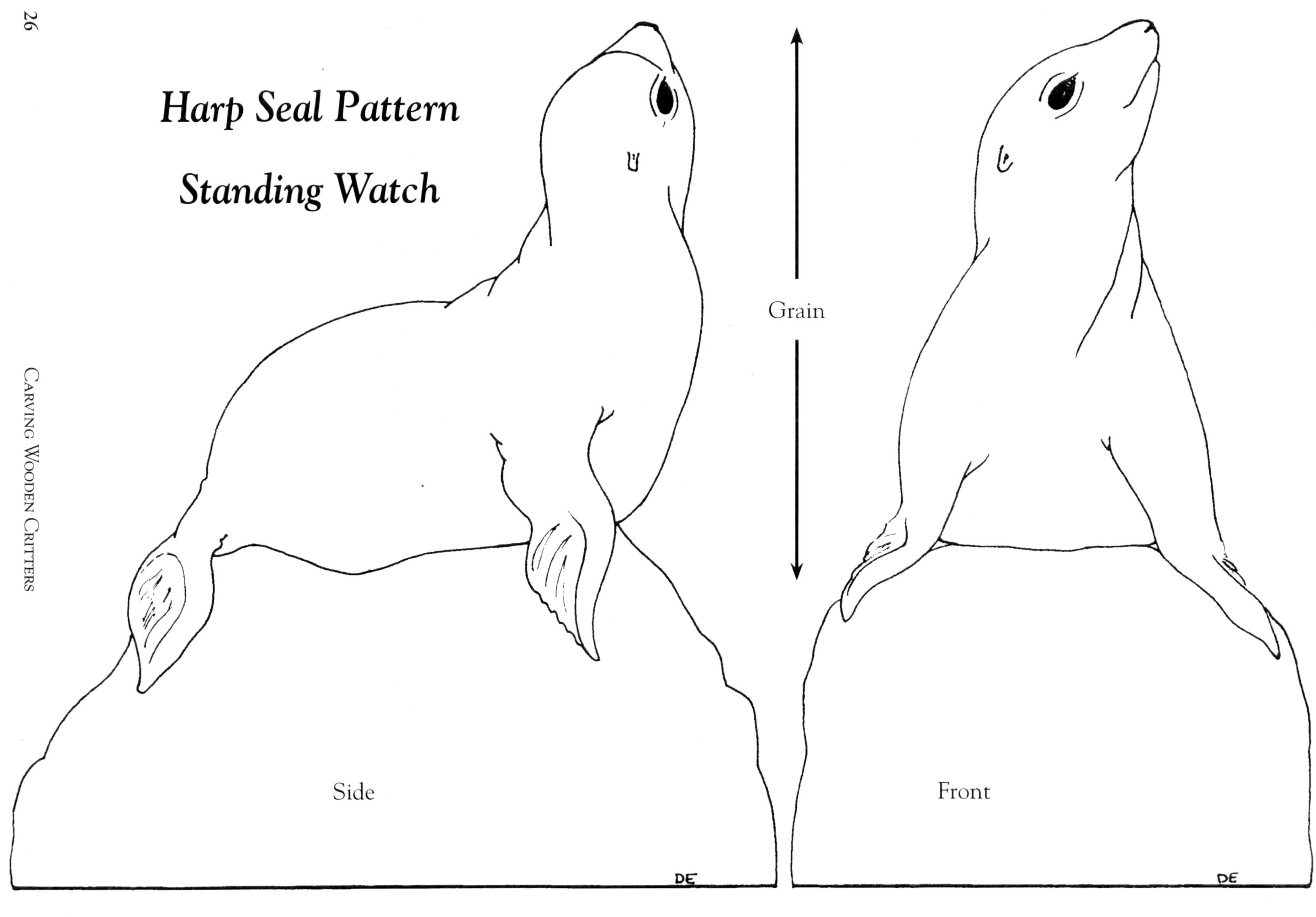
Harp Seal Pattern
Standing Watch
Grain
Side
Front
DE
DE

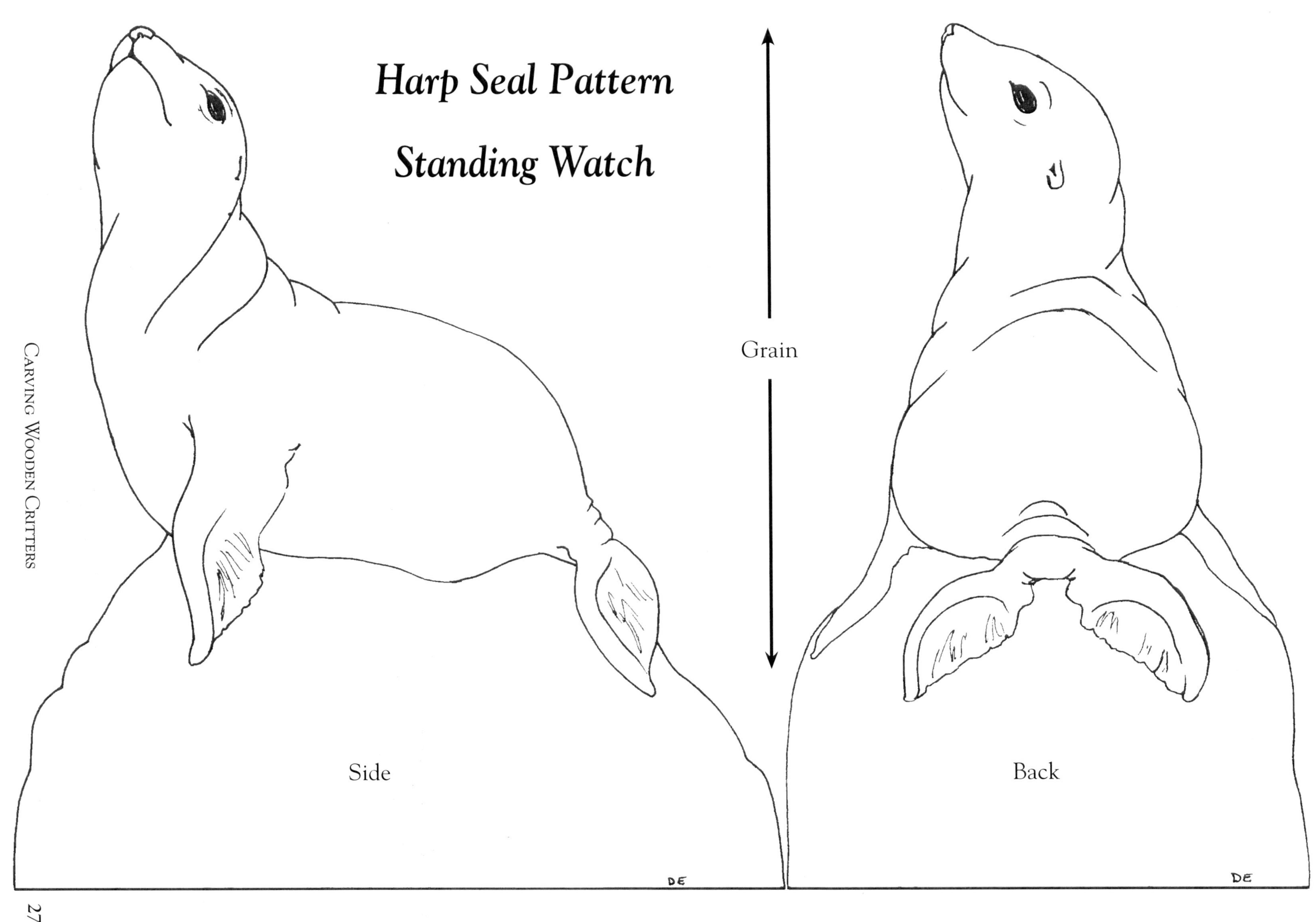

Harp Seal Pattern
Standing Watch
Grain
Side
Back
DE
DE

Panda Pattern

Big Buddy

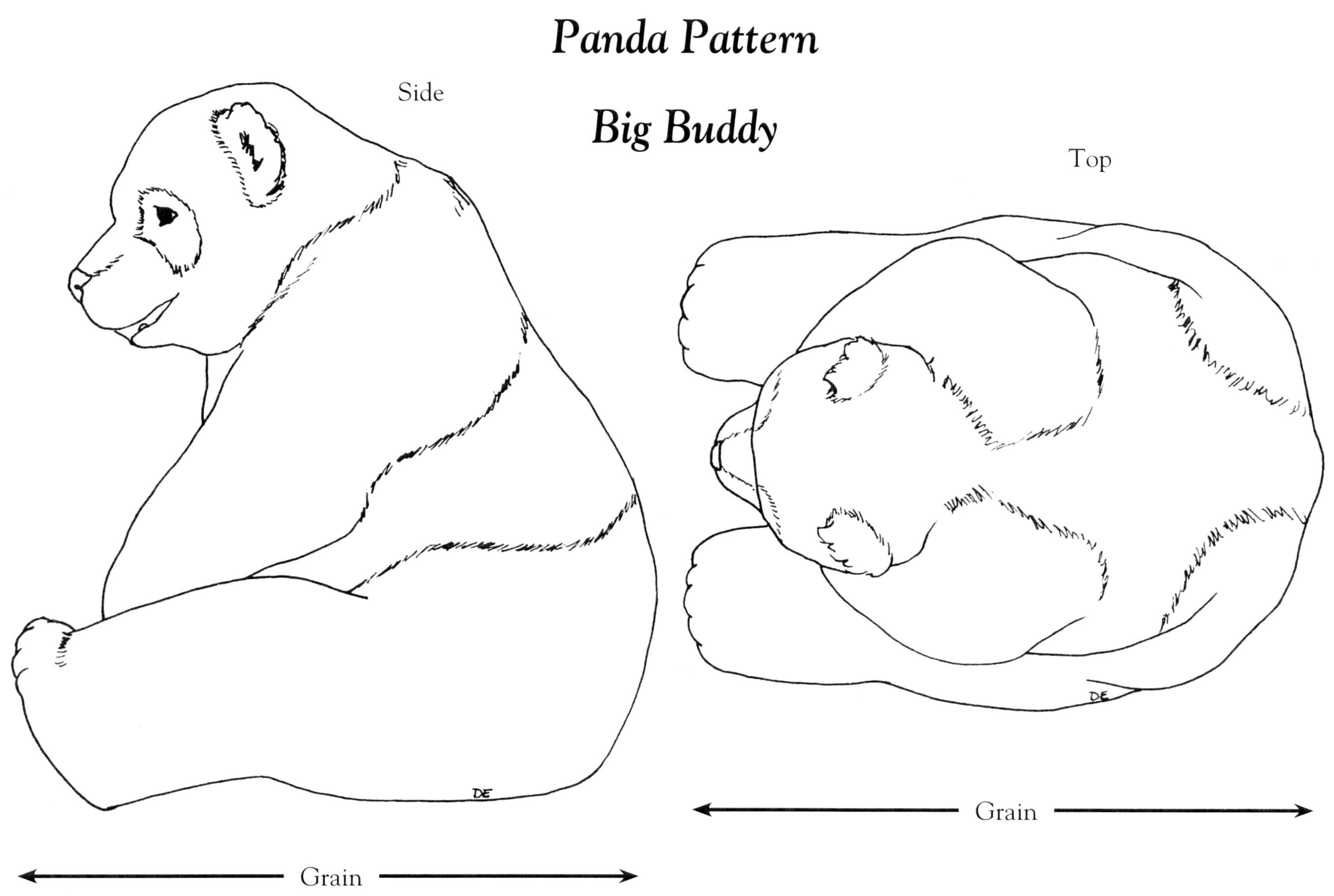

Panda Pattern

Big Buddy

River Otter Pattern
Hangin' Out

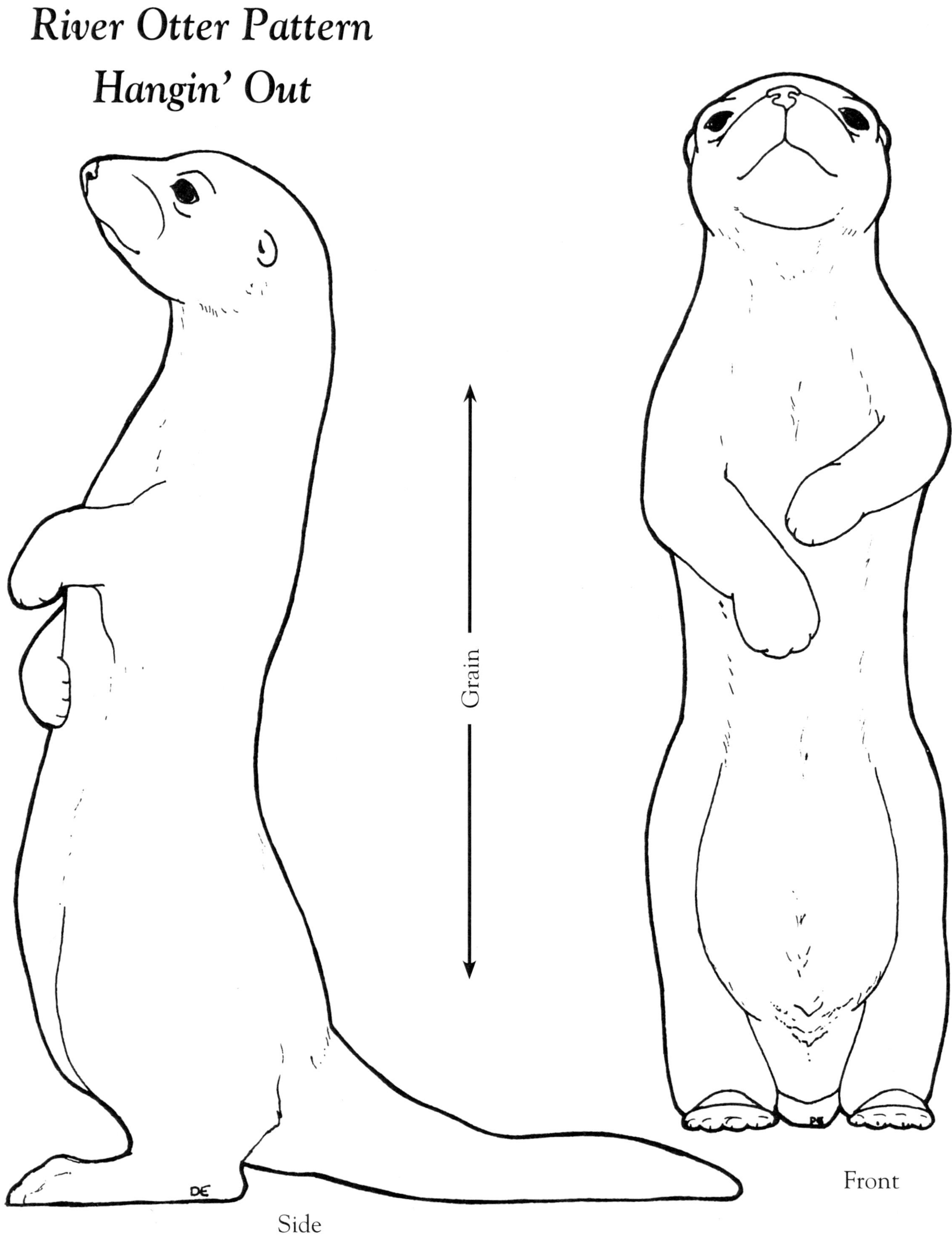

    Carving Wooden Critters

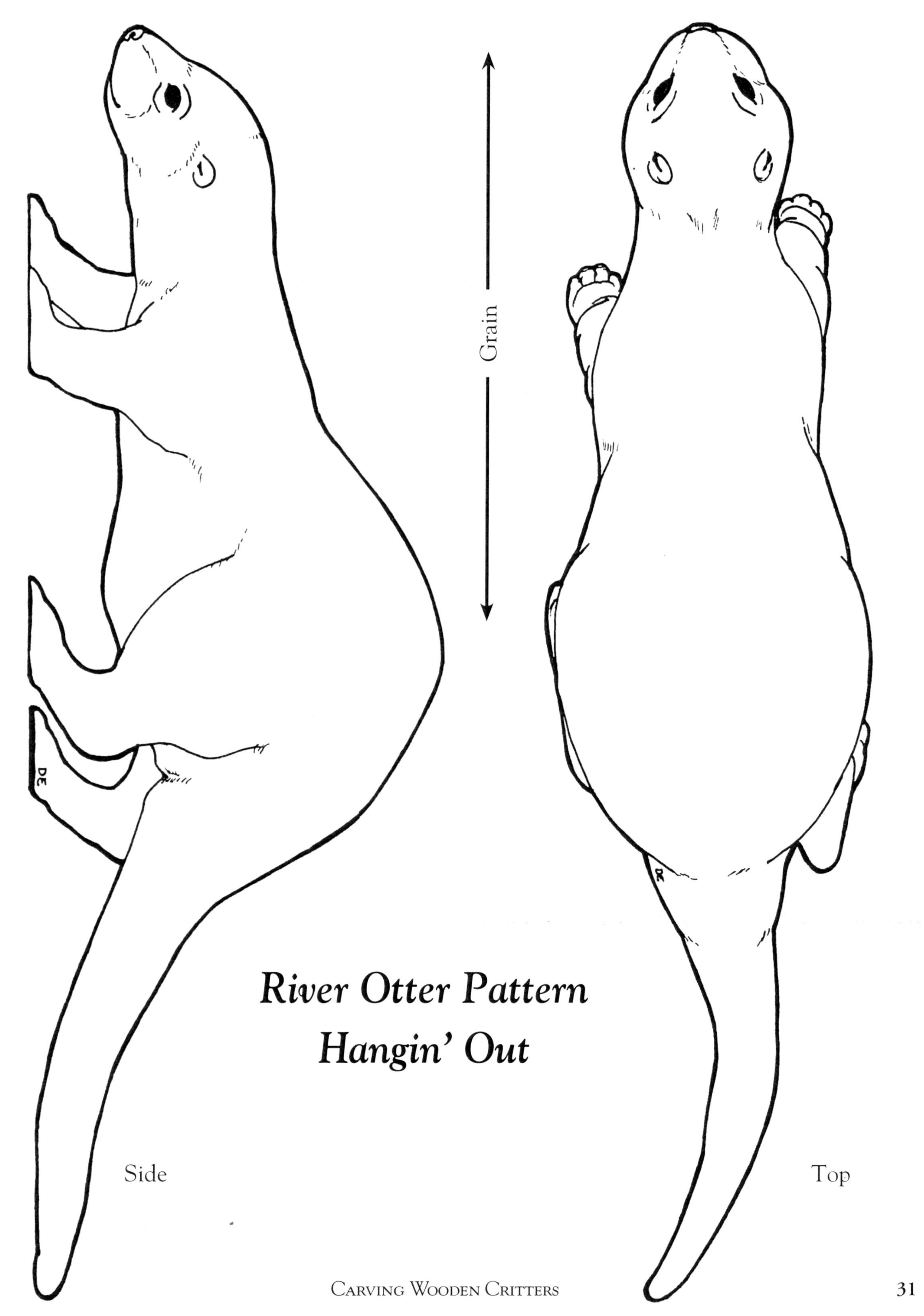

Grain
River Otter Pattern
Hangin' Out
Side
Top

Chipmunk Pattern

Having a Bite

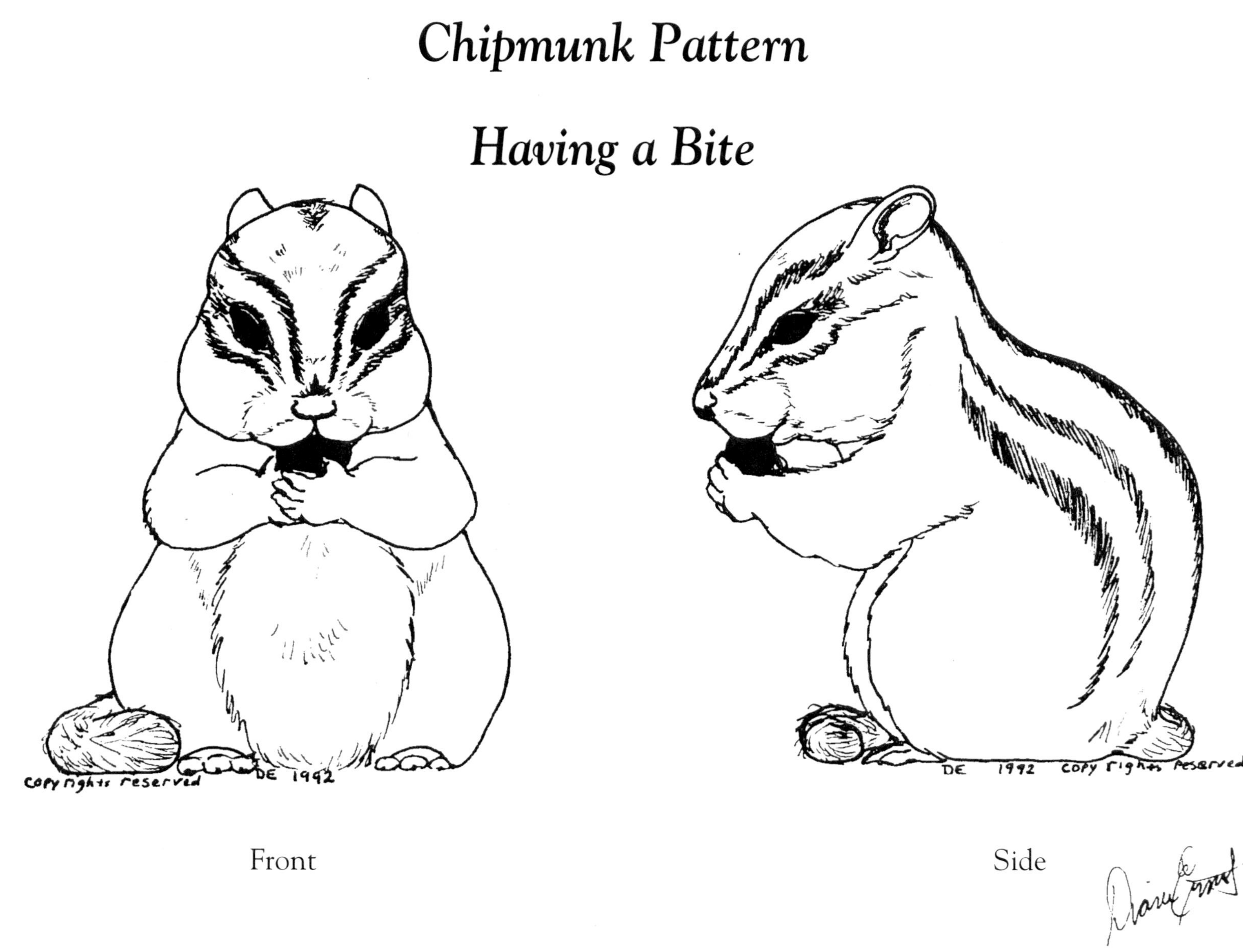

Front

Side

Chipmunk Pattern
Sitting Pretty

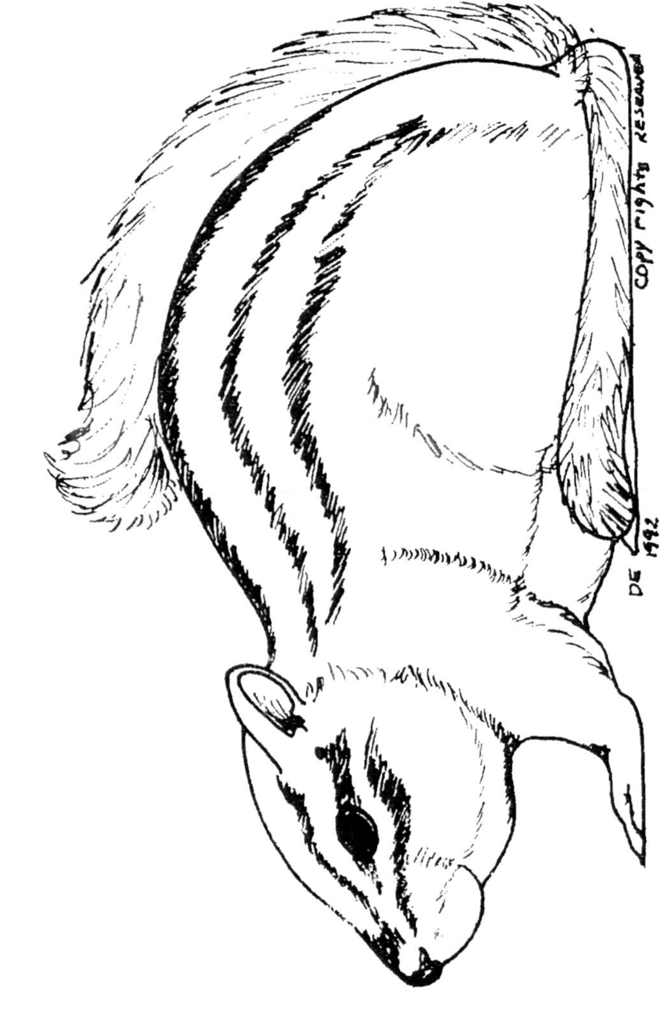

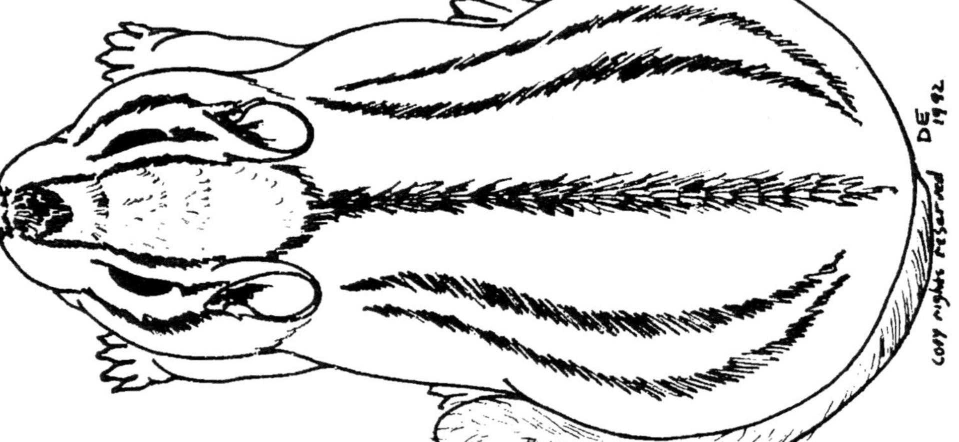

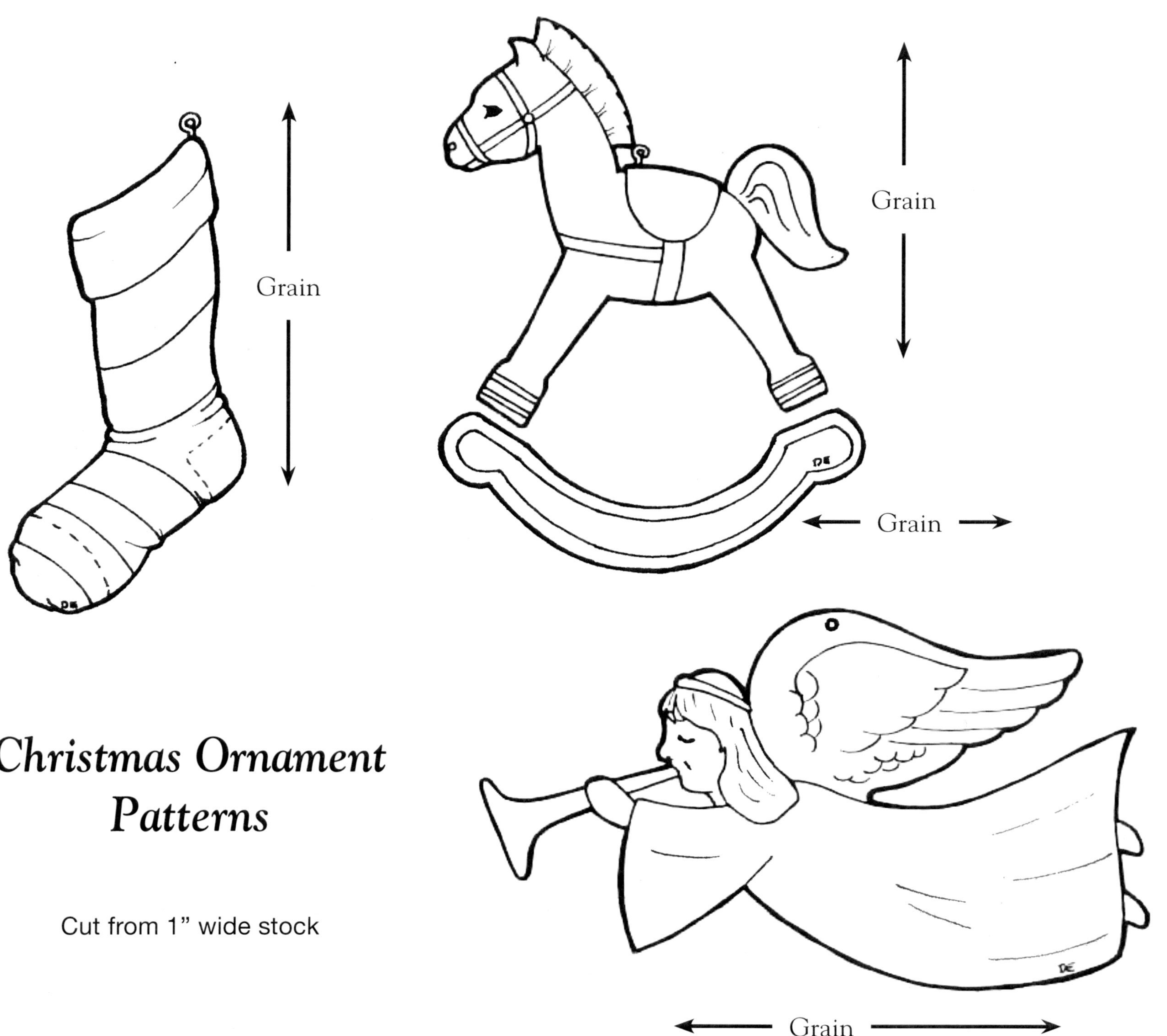

Christmas Ornament Patterns

Cut from 1" wide stock